A-Z
The Universe in Me

Positive affirmations for realizing our unlimited potential

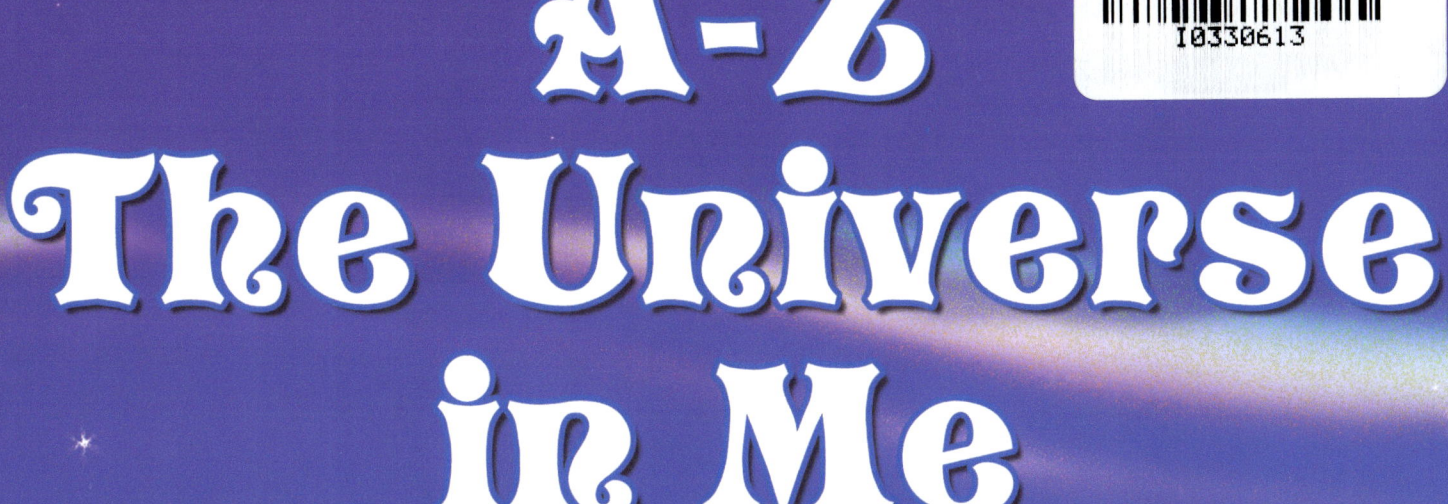

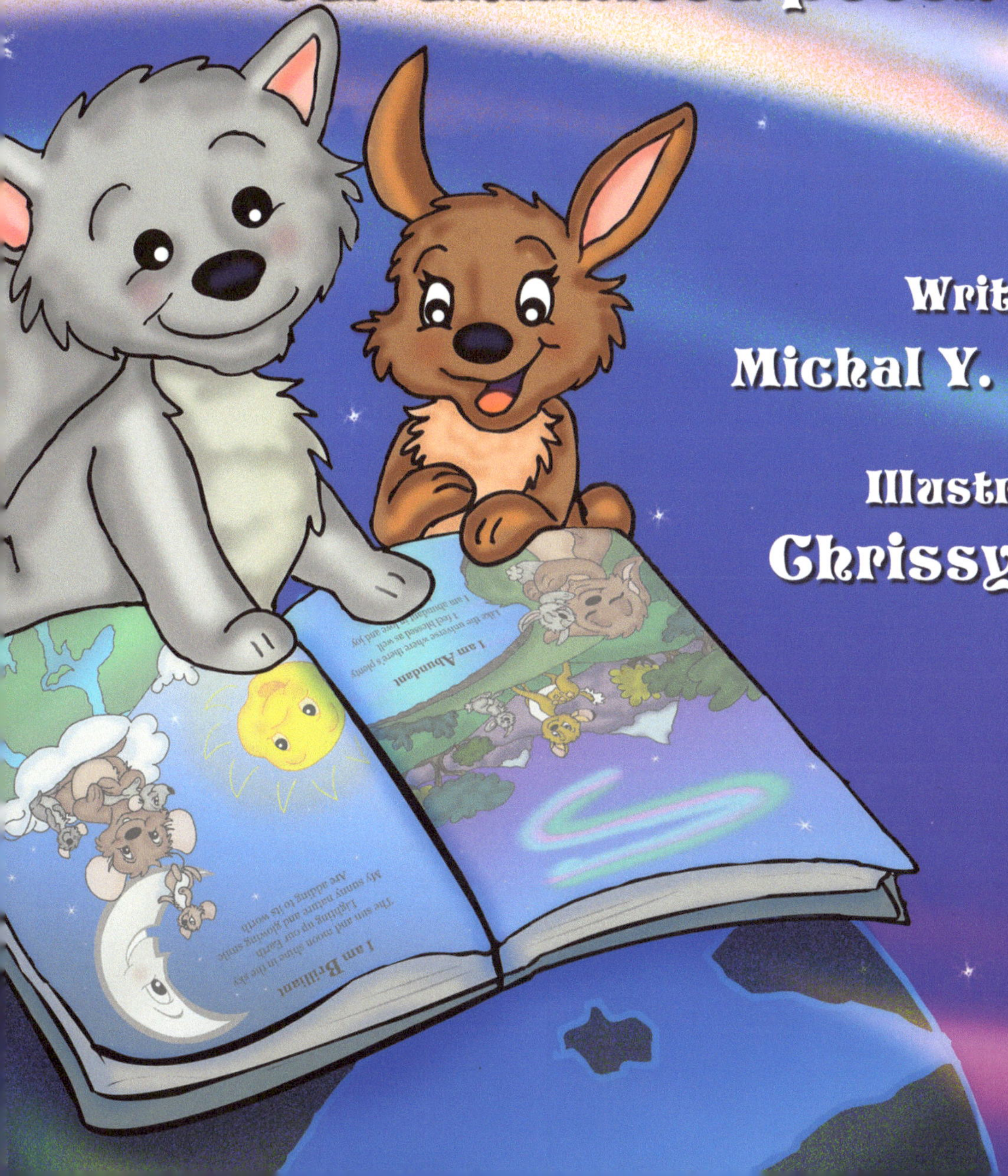

Written by
Michal Y. Noah, Ph.D.

Illustrated by
Chrissy Fanslau

Text and Illustrations Copyright © 2011 by Michal Y. Noah

All rights reserved. No part of this publication may be reproduced, distributed, or transmitted in any form or by any means, including photocopying, recording, or other electronic or mechanical methods, without the prior written permission of the publisher, except in the case of brief quotations embodied in critical reviews and cer‹tain other noncommercial uses permitted by copyright law. For permission requests, write to the publisher, addressed "Attention: Permissions Coordinator," at the address below.

A Magical World in You, Inc.
Huntingdon Valley, PA 19006
www.michalynoah.com

Hardcover ISBN 978-0-9908394-0-8
Paperback ISBN 978-0-9908394-1-5

Library of Congress Control Number: 2014917279

This is a work of fiction. Names, characters, businesses, places, events and incidents are either the products of the author's imagination or used in a fictitious manner. Any resemblance to actual persons, living or dead, or actual events is purely coincidental.

Ordering Information:

Quantity sales. Special discounts are available on quantity purchases by corporations, associations, and others. For details, contact the publisher at the address above.

Printed in the United States of America.

DEAR PARENTS AND TEACHERS

Hi, My name is Michal and I am passionate about bringing out the best in people, especially children who have so much untapped potential that it is a joy when it unfolds! It is my goal that kids should have higher self-esteem and self-confidence to empower them and help them to realize that true power comes from within.

Affirmations are a great way to achieve that! This book **'A-Z, the Universe in Me'** is a collection of short poems of positive affirmations that I have composed especially for children to hear and to enjoy, to sing and to repeat.

When you, as a parent, grandparent, or teacher read them out aloud to young kids, you will realize that these are more than just affirmations; the poems contain the principles and philosophies that I have picked up during a decade of study and research. The book represents my way of viewing and living life!

Our self-talk has a definite effect on the attitudes and outcomes in our lives. What we think, we create! Our thoughts, words and beliefs are powerful creating tools that are at work all the time, whether we realize it or not. Affirmations are very effective with young children because they are in tune with their inner power and emphasizing positive thoughts and feelings gives children the self-confidence and positive outlook, which helps them create joyful experiences.

The simple poems are written in an easy to recite style. Drawing parallels from nature, they focus on the fact that all the qualities from A-Z in the Universe are in every child.

Guidelines on using this book: -

1. The poems should be read out in a positive and enthusiastic way.

2. Affirmations can be a powerful tool when the words "I AM" are emphasized. Encourage children to use them often, e.g. "I am kind," or "I am grateful."

3. Affirmations works best when emotionalized and repeated daily. Singing and reciting the poems are a fun way to evoke emotion, which is very important to make affirmations effective.

4. Reading the poems aloud at bedtime is a wonderful way to end the day.

5. Children learn by observation and imitation; parents are powerful role models who can positively influence children if they indulge in positive self-talk themselves. If parents make it a point to use constructive language that reflects self-confidence, love, trust, and abundance it is the best gift that they can give their children, for this is sure to counteract the negative and self-limiting thoughts that children face everyday. Affirmations, combined with positive emotions, are a powerful way to help us and our children manifest a joyful life.

6. Finally, I believe that the reader as well as the listener will benefit from reading these poems.

Wishing you lots of joy and abundance,

-Michal Y Noah

This book was written just for YOU
To remind you who you are
And the wonderful things you can have, be, and do
Believe in yourself, know that it's true
Greatness is really all about you
So say it out loud, repeat it, and as you do
You will feel the Universe's unlimited potential
Working through you too!

I am Abundant

Like the universe where there's plenty
I feel blessed as well
I am abundant in love and joy
Anyone can tell

I am Brilliant

The sun and moon shine in the sky
Lighting up our Earth
My sunny nature and glowing smile
Are adding to its worth

I am Confident

Confidently sings the bird
Fearlessly swims the fish
I know that I too
Can achieve whatever I wish

I am Determined

Trees grow and seeds sprout
Sure of what they do
I am a child of the universe
Determined to succeed too

I am Excellent

I have wonderful qualities
That you have too
I am joyful and affectionate
I am fantastic just like you

I am Free

Like the wind that freely blows
And the flower that easily grows
I am unstoppable, I am free
To choose who I want to be.

I am Grateful

I give thanks to the universe
For all the nice people I've met
For all the magical gifts I now have
And those I am sure to get

I am Hopeful

I trust my heart, I am full of hope
I know there is magic within me
As a lovable child of the universe
I expect that the best will come to be

I am Infinite

An infinite bundle of gifts am I
Like every other girl and boy
A treasure of love and sweetness
For myself and others to enjoy

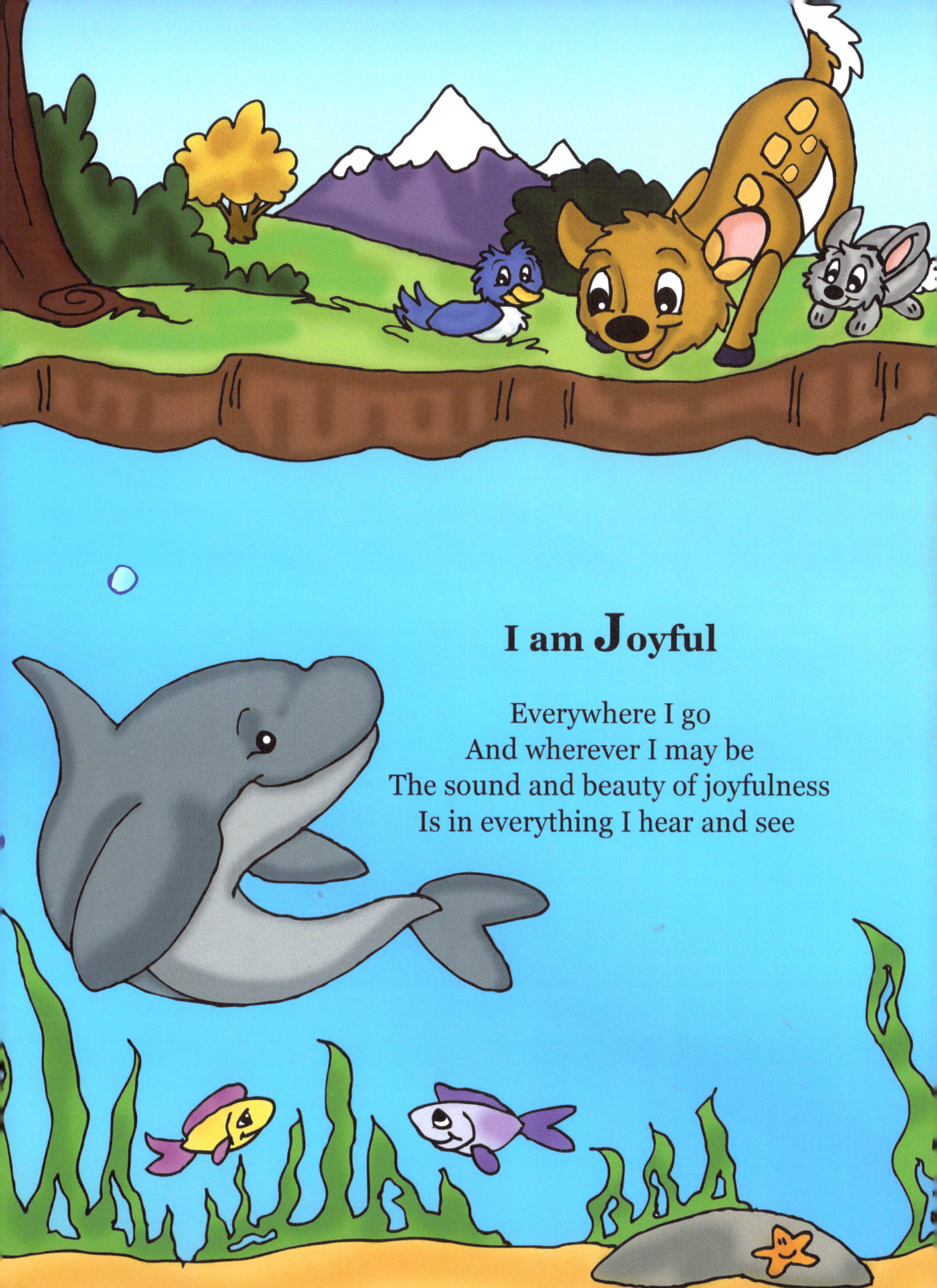

I am Joyful

Everywhere I go
And wherever I may be
The sound and beauty of joyfulness
Is in everything I hear and see

I am Kind

I have beautiful eyes
Only good in others I find
I have beautiful lips
They only say words that are kind

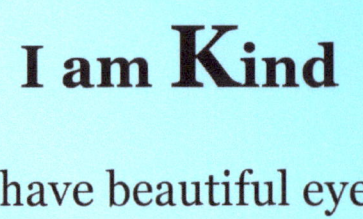

I am Magnificent

From such a tiny acorn
Grows a mighty oak tree
It's magnificent, you must agree
Awesome, just like you and me

I am Nurturing

I plant some flowers and treat them with care
Giving them water and lots of fresh air
A lovely bird or a cute little cat
Will get my love, be sure of that

I am Oneness

The beauty of a flower
The strength of a tree
The brightness of the sky
Are also in me

I am Perfect

The universe is perfect
Every galaxy, planet and star
Every bird, flower and fish
And lovely little me, by far

I think Quality thoughts

My mind is like a garden
Every positive thought is a seed
When I nourish it with love and care
I get great results – it's just what I need

I am Responsible

For everything that I say
For whatever I think, feel and do
I am the only one responsible
It feels great, yes, It's true

I am Sharing

The sun never gets tired
Of sharing its warmth and light
I share with others whatever I have
When I give, it feels just right

I am Thoughtful

Looking at an insect crawling up the tree
Listening to the buzzing sound of a bee
Thoughtful and kind and so very nice
That's truly a perfect description of me

I am Unique

I am so unique, I am so special
Yes, I know it is true
I have my own special way
To do the things I like to do

I am Valuable

I am special, an incredible little child
More precious than diamonds or gold
I am valued and loved for what I am
My qualities are too many to be told

I am Wise

The little ant is wise and strong
It's plain for all to see
Although I'm still young in age
There is great wisdom within me

I am X-traordinary

From crawling on the ground
To flying in the clear blue sky
A caterpillar turned into a beautiful butterfly
How extraordinary! Just like you and I

I say 'Yes' to success

When I face a challenge
I keep on saying YES
I know that if I keep on trying
It will bring me great success

I am Zestful

I find joy in little things
I love smiles and laughter
There are wonderful things all around me
They are blessings for now and ever after

Other Books by Michal Noah, Ph.D.

The Magic Tree

I'll See You in My Dreams

Sparkles